Savage Survivals
amid modern suavity

Also by Andrew Duncan:

Poetry

In a German Hotel
Knife Cuts the Water
Cut Memories and False Commands
From the Kitchen Floor
Sound Surface
Alien Skies
Skeleton Looking at Chinese Pictures
Switching and Main Exchange
Pauper Estate
Anxiety Before Entering a Room: Selected Poems
Surveillance and Compliance
The Imaginary in Geometry

Criticism

The Failure of Conservatism in Modern British Poetry
Centre and Periphery in Modern British Poetry
Origins of the Underground:
       The Occlusion of British Poetry 1932-1977

As editor

Don't Start Me Talking: Interviews with Contemporary Poets
(with Tim Allen)

Andrew Duncan

Savage Survivals

amid modern suavity

Shearsman Books
Exeter

Published in the United Kingdom in 2006 by
Shearsman Books Ltd
58 Velwell Road
Exeter EX4 4LD

ISBN-13   978-1-905700-03-5

ISBN-10   1-905700-03-2

Acknowledgements
'Weapons Form' was published in *Oasis* (entire)
'Extreme Computing' was published in *Cul de Qui*
'Andy-the-German' was published in *CCCP Review* and in a Salt
anthology.

Contents

"I want what you want, human boy.'
— from *Dead Girls*, by Richard Calder

'The third part of your brain – do you know where it is?' 'Wrapped around the solenoid in my central body cavity.'
— from *Demon with a Glass Hand*,
episode of 'The Outer Limits'

"Careful inquiry should be made to discover the existence of such a system; where it is not in general use it is sometimes used by one sex only, preserved in the memory of old people, used in ritual, or guarded as a sacred art. In each system note what sort of ideas can be expressed by signs. Give a full vocabulary if possible; if not, typical examples. Can connected narratives or speech be expressed? Are there signs for 'beginning' and 'ending' a message, to indicate a question, or otherwise to qualify or explain any sign or group of signs? Are the signs used as an accompaniment to spoken language? Are they used in hunting, war, bargaining?"
— excerpt from *Notes and Queries on Anthropology*

Acoustic Shock

1. It was 1964, or 1965. My family and I were on the beach at West Bay, in Dorset, and I saw the ruins of a harbour strewn around. The haven had been built with big concrete blocks, each weighing perhaps a ton. I could not see how the sea had torn them up. They were cast carelessly around as if they had been dropped from mid-air. It was a new harbour and it was as if the sea had refused to accept it.

2. In 2002, I read about this process. As concrete sets, it shrinks slightly and develops tiny cracks. When a wave breaks on concrete close to the airline, it pushes the air already in these gaps in the fabric. The air is a very narrow column with a huge force driving it — like a hammer hitting a nail. The smaller the nail of water, the more force it exerts at its point. Because it has nowhere to go, the air becomes hard. Temporarily, the speed of the air is the speed of the wave times the ratio between the size of the crack and the size of the wave. It attacks the boundaries between them and makes the cracks join up.

Blast, draft, syllable
spirit blowing in the mass —
the Atlantic breathing through a crack
The aulos is the pipe through which the god
fills *the soft wrapping of the tender membranes*
hydraulically jacked & jittered shook &
shattered in structural hiss

The sea knows nothing
and is experimenting with an island
It grows calm behind the stone-fold, the shelter
It records its microstructure, says
but is mimesis *knowledge*?

Rolling, rolling
The block is teetering on its own flaw
tree wrenching out its roots one by one

All structure is subliminal
knowledge seeps out on substance flowing away
through cycles. when a wave disintegrates
it slows down the moon

The grapnel of vocal air
growing slowly through blind slab
to copy a precise design
splitting pore from grip

Fingers of the ocean blow down the pipes
to see if chips fly back
to hear its own roar, sharpened
Fife stops burnt at the breaking point

The sea is softer than seaweed
it knows nothing
it knows the shape of things to molecular level
It has no memory and no limbs
it has the concept of a bomb
a floating mine with sensory spikes

The harbour is a crystal that rings
and destroys itself. A sound
is drawing architecture
It wants months

A capillary fulcrum
sketching itself
with shattering fingers
grains as holdfasts

siege gear, slighting-wall, new ordinance
of space
pistol chamber exit wound
rocker switch detonated by tone
hydraulic cement hydraulically slighted
& set aside
spray pits salivate rust

the storming party escalade
the breach blown underwater
decked in white lace
brought off in sunken barges

the spiracles fingers of air
scrolled up like spills
pushing as if through the stomae of leaves
Qualmwasser
the pistol or fountain-jet
a thrill that spurts out of the back
of someone's head

a lizard of stone whose parts don't join up
in a puzzle the Channel will solve
a flicker of spring limbs
a lizard of air that's no longer there

waves sledge dredging for the last edges of
integrity
hand shake grip sliding seams start
the sea whirls the rocks around its head
to daze them
house-sized gravel rolled by a stream
frame capture
stone swimming through water
frame capture
water breaking under strain
frame capture
motion gives way to structure

The concrete block crawls a few feet and then gets tired
the shoreline is the ruin of all past shorelines
the surface of the shear is solid & impervious

the engines of order overthrown
by wavelines the cults of static power
towering in blocks of arrested will
metabolised by birds breathing

as tall buildings rush
outwards, shuddering wall, storms
raze the empire of sound with ribbons
of air, nails of water

Crossing the Border Hills in an Aeroplane

a sublime fall. a crash. a sea of howl.
a horse of air. a ray or strut
crossing from the swelling ground
to the surface of my eye
a sweep or feather
poised over laws, grains, and cleughs

My great great great grandfather's parish
My great great great great grandfather's parish
My great great great grand-uncle's parish

a lens seven miles long and two feet wide
diverging as distance draws out
lifting up an entire tract of hills
in the shape of the cabin window

at the bottom of this shaft
I would tread on the straws
on a tussock that sinks in and bends
as I counter-swerve left and swerve right
a kind of capillary bounce exper
imental quaking of my pelvis to recover
straight stance. on a nod. slip shod.
toes clenching and fingertips waving
triplash arpeggio of vertebral cogs.

This godlike seeing
is starvation to the skin,
a blank and sublime state, lifted out,
rare to vanishing, I can see other islands
covered in polished granite & crystal cities
covered in cubes, domes, and cylinders
covered in birch, covered in olives.

The lying snow sharp in the air lens
white on brown winter heath foliage
a whole language of gloss patches
repetitive and unseizable
like a camouflage pelt, toned
from blanket to single clumps on stalks
a map of warmth, wind shelter in brown
a map of altitude, clear lower slopes
with running water we see as deep cracks

Thin air lens catching process of the hill
struck dumb by its becoming, voiced
by the repetition of its fellows,
thing making hills the hills can't
be taken away from, from deep air
deep stair

Taxi-ing in west over Leith Docks
with thoughts of the Malt Shovel barrelhead on twisting steep street
ovens swallowing ripe barley in the brewery out on Lothian Road
don't forget to catch me fill me with the full Eighty Shilling

Weapons Form with Music

a patriotic outburst of thanks to Mr Brian HOLTON for his oversetting the Chinese outlaw novel, Water Margin [水滸傳 *or* Shuihu Zhuàn], *with 70 chapters and 108 heroes, into the SCOTTISH language; sampling passages from Sir Thomas URQUHART and the* Lives of the Presbyterian Saints

(1)
Turning in at the red pillars under the fine old mountains
The brief swarthy outlaw drank the wine
And, as it found its courses,
Called out, Waiter!
Bring me an ink-stone and a brush!
I feel like writing an epic!

He set out the treachery of Claverhouse and King Charles,
The corruption of officials in the Millet Bureau,
The virtues of hazel nuts, watercress, and badger fat,
The reasons for the flatness of Strathclyde.

Insolent yamen runners, hawkers of faked tiger bones,
New Right politicians, reactionary clerics,
prepotent landowners, Jacobite papal knights,
conniving lawyers, English patronage cliques,
country and western pubs, ley line whitterers,
strict tempo poets, entry-level sociolinguists — all
would be practice for his new sword patterns.

As the tips of the forest lightly swished and tossed,
He said, What passes are these, when
Writing about outlaws is almost a crime
Because of all the trees being hushed up?

(2)

The Glasgow avant-garde redesign the Campsie Fells; Sung
Chiang chastises an insufficiently courteous hashed-meat vendor

A blue sword in a white hand.

At the very point where sky and sword-tip meet, appears
a black dot, rich and splendid, with all
the qualities of the blood, milk and ink of the Dalriads
dense and perfumed as a summer night

a very rich, stiff, finely-ground ink
— made with very old and well-matured oil

blood wringing with Qi
from hours of noble exercise
swallowing air as if washing in it

milk from a cow licentiously loosed
on the lushest of buttery meadows blushing from a midsummer
            flood

this is the black dot of ethical focus, it
is brought into being by truth spoken
and heard on both sides

(3)
Deirdre and Naoise take refuge from Conchobar in the Border Hills;
Pai Shung and Sung Chiang train a corps of slit gong players

Wet petals clinging to a pomegranate.

Sung Chiang applies
a tab of LSD under each eyelid
left and right
and sticks a martial arts video on—
Five Elements Ninja.
Indeed, we are not in the city
said the Daylight Rat.

(4)

Jade Lion gives up editing an avant-garde poetry magazine and joins the outlaws of the marsh; the unjustly banished heroes drink lager to excess

I'd just taken my giro to the Post Office
That day I slaked my thirst
In a way I never will forget
The eight heroes of Liang Shan Po just walked up to the rail
And struck Bar Attitude Number 4—
I didn't know that then.
They were so cool the whole room froze
The beer at the tap stopped pouring
The smoke in the air stopped drifting
The flames in the hearth stopped flickering
The ceiling fan slowed down to single rotary strokes
Which were the knocking of my heart

The waves of sex and Qi made me stagger.
It felt like fear but I was drunk on it
I felt my old self die
I knew this old town and its syllabic metres could never hold me
I knew I would grow up to go stravaiging,
Hanging bishops, impaling dragoons, chasing tigers. Things like
        that.
It wasn't the usual gloom in the Subdued Fiends Hall.

The heroes with black hair and blue eyes were wearing
double dragon belt buckles made from Arctic copper
high boots made of unpolished soft fawn calfskin
shirts of linen dyed with saffron
red ear-lapping fox-fur caps with blue waving aigrettes
cloaks made of blue and gold tassels
cherkesskas with chest bandoliers of burnished brass rifle cartridges

sgians with glass pommels in leather sheaths on gold braid galloons
penannular bronze cloakclasps with inlaid affronted writhing beasts
T-shirts with big Iggy transfers printed on them
and leopard-skin pillbox hats.

They were carrying lost WS Graham books and original Elmore
          James acetates
— casual like. That's when I said to myself,
these guys are no on the Minimum Wage,
Any cooler, and your joints seize up.
Hey Rodolfo
I'll have what they're having
I went to the games console just to practise standing, a bit.
I walked up and I stared at them real hard.
Is it true you're the lads killed Ni Erh?

We were expecting you, said Lu Ta.

(5)

Lu Ta observes the movements of animals on the slopes of Misty Mountain; Zen Ping uses his deep cleansing herbal clay masque

They compared the polychrome clothes of the Celtic missionaries
known as the Striped Ones
with the multiple ragged robes of the roaming Buddhists—
cloaks filled with the virtues of the teachers who had filled them

They contrasted the 49 basic animal forms of Wu Chin
with the martial arts learnt at Scathach's academy on Skye

They put on one side the arhats wandering over the Himalayas
        and the deserts of Tibet
on the other, a visit to *sifu* Ian Hamilton Finlay

(6)

Welcome Rain Meets the Flying Prince; Black Whirlwind Fights with White Fish

As the 108 heroes were sauntering out of the only gay bar in
        Inverness
they were recognised by the grocer's wife.
The news was all over the north-east
before the last bus had left for the villages.

(7)
Shih Ch'ien sets fire to the blue cloud tower; Wu Yung takes Ta Ming Fu with a subtle plan

He tied the two brothers' heads to the fins of the chariot
and turned the jingling horses' heads for home.

(8)
'From Zenith to Pupil': a Northern Summer

fleeting actinic magentas

the smallest rim of a night you
could catch in your hand and
hang upon a tree

sheets of soluble purples
phantoms in gold leaf
staring serried in a dandelion halo of blur
thin air- basking in the unslanting unquenched
they watch to replete themselves with rarety
the mill of beams
its Hyperborean candour
a subtle gush of serotonin
pure Time, the draught of winning speed.
A deflector to cup the core as it shatters—

a trajectory
copied by the warriors in bird masks
brains soaked in living light
drawn along the meridian
like a crane along its flight:
a ray from a small soundless star

stress breaks into sound, a hai!
a universe of knowledge, before the
eye for only the frail
anatomy of a moment,
developed
by flourishes of straight and oblique lines,
bursts and scatters, a new plane joins itself up

the light sighs and shifts in quality

(9)
In Caledonia Dysarta

Dysart, the Irish-Latin pronunciation of desert
a solitude found by the holy in Egypt:
depopulated and free from deceit
in the northwest there are no drylands nor scorpions
they resited to hills, swamps, and rocky shores

The vigil of standing in the Tweed all night long, or
the Dispersed Limbs Form
sitting in a cloud of midges
dodging all of them

Vigils of disenchantment.
Outside the cut lines of street and plough
fevers and dreams native and demonic
to be shorn by watches of the spiritual elite

The pioneer claims his plot and lifts bright iron.
Root tangles that twist and plunge into the ground,
snaking, radiating, controverting,
branched lashed and cross-braced, closed in clay.
Straight furrows that twist overnight.
He starts sleeping in trees, loses power of speech.

Bones shaking
out of standing water like a shine
the myth blackens their flesh
a viral tape endemic and tutelar
entraining the brain for its recurrence
speaks for the place and
belongs to us all

heresy at neuromuscular level
one day you wake cold and well
after thirty years of error
in one chest of foul papers
crabbed and jittered script

In the Rough Bounds the vagrant and extravagant
spilled fullness of nut-eaters, convulsives, heretics,
regressives covered in thick hair, Cameronians,
antinomians, *geilt* men running along the tops of trees,
hermits, messengers speaking in unknown languages,
men that fancied themselves to be
women, beasts, trees, stones, pitchers, glasses, angels,
Method actresses, Poll Tax resisters, open field poets,
receiving and making the signs of wolves, the dual series
of sounds and movements.

(**10**)
The Hand of Claverhouse; A lay of the Scottish Cavaliers

In May of 1685 it was the Killing Times for the readers of the Bible.

This made Claverhouse to examine those whom he had taken to be his guides thorow the muirs, if ever they heard this John Brown preach: they answered, 'No, no, he was never a preacher.' He said, 'If he has never preached, meikle has he prayed in his time.'

He said to John, 'Go to your prayers, for you shall immediately die.' When ended, Claverhouse said, 'Take goodnight of your wife and children.' Brown kissed his wife and bairns, and wished purchased and promised blessings to be multiplied on them, and his blessing.

Claverhouse ordered six soldiers to shoot him;
the most part of the bullets came upon his head,
which scattered his brains upon the ground.
Claverhouse said to his wife,
'What thinkest thou of thy husband now, woman?'

She said, 'I thought ever much good of him, and as much now as
        ever.'
He said, 'It were but justice to lay thee beside him.
To man I can be answerable,
and for God, I will take him in my own hand.'

Claverhouse mounted his horse, and marched,
and left her with the corpse of her dead husband lying there;
she set the bairn upon the ground, and gathered his brains,
and tied up his head, and straighted his body,
and covered him with her plaid,
and sat down and wept over him.

(11)
Cum furca et fovea

Where sweet turns to salt
A river with no shore and the Tilbury hulks.
Without rights, to save rights
laying heads on boards, the lading of Highlandmen
sworn to the wrong king.
They linger where tide and current lap and tussle.
Whose justice? which rationality?
The founding of panegyric in heroic contests
Whose memory shapes the ideals of the young.

The smell of mud and tar.
The current holds the tide and looses.
Disobedience in the will and distraction by passion.
The sowing of the wilderness with a seed of wild men
The thoroughfare of ships and lane of trade
Borne up by water and held down with chains
Gibbet and pit: the graces of air and water

If Canada is warm, and
Pennsylvania has woods with no heir.
In the Essex reaches, in the birth-passage of Empire
Where dysentery's fleet rides by malaria's shore
Cheeks red as foxgloves and hair yellow as primroses
The strategy of Rome or the clemency of Westminster.
True words ceasing where the buildings start
The tide pens in the current and
Forgets itself.

(12)
Weapons form with invective; the Heroes face the Knights of Saint
Columba in the Open Field and are Worsted by a Ruse

Tailored, nonchalant, fork-tailed, eight foot by four,
a Tory devil, greenish skin puffed by poison sacs,
the thief of truth in plain sight,
blurred by paralysing waves of disinformational sound
is seizing the soft points in your nervous system

First draw on the Deep Emptiness
and give way to the demonic principle

Go back to his source material to convict him of pretention,
    chauvinism, partiality, and poor scholarship
kick him in the head

Suggest he hasn't understood Hegel
find his rhythm and disconcert it all over,
disturb his moments of gathering

While drawing out the core fantasies on which his logic rests
use the double-handed, Northern Marches, vertebra-shearing,
    "glowing rim", expressive-brushstroke backsweep

He edits your speech for broadcast, making you
a palsied, hot-headed thick-tongue.
Ignore his victories. treat your mistakes with kindness
alonge a stoccade up and under his ribs

Employ jeers, squibs, flouts, buls, quips, taunts, whims
and clenches
bring out the potato peeler and let him know you mean to use it

Contraposture his Wards
swap his inner organs around
transqualify him into the Numbness of a Pageant

He fields the DOD-contracted, MIT-linked, white-supremacist
    Foundation moneyed, geopolitical nightshade think-tanks
the CIA's soft and sonorous parts
their views on Scotland

A favour network of courts, bars, and TV stations
builds a wordless consensus
in which you are comically cut off
from the reason ending where they say;
slight his falsifyings
break measure to destroy his flow
'you are a coward, a bourgeois, and an anglophile'

Make him breathless with *Aufhebung*
crouch in the immovable low-gravity stance

Untwine his founding metaphors and insist they are ornaments
take his centre of gravity and hurl it outwards

He projects an entire artificial landscape
lets restaurants, spacious grounds, and grand interiors
aestheticise a whole status order;
adopt the posture of knowing how language really works
find the cluster of nerves at the groin

Cite your own many years of field research
a two-finger jab to the pharynx

He takes flight through a hundred shifts of shape;
expose his links to an interpenetrative elite
of merchant bankers and chauvinistic Oxford dons; adapt
the Excruciation called "Two Apricots"

Mercilessly cite semioticists of the University of Tartu
tell him it's twilight for the Deep Pigs

Expose his loyalties as complicity and his glosses as duplicity
open him from chin to trouser

(13)
Satellite mapping land and lordship with Ronnie Laing

Up on the satellite swinging over Caithness
we felt the landscape wrap itself around us
the mylar screens imitating a whole horizon
total green, total blue, total spray-white immersing us
still downloading data to the land station.
Marking-on the boundaries of the great estates,
Peter said, 900 families own four-fifths of Scotland,
You can't see lordship on this camera
and tests suggest you can't touch it either
It's something we all agree to
or else disagree

Learning a map of blocks on motion
through the maze of overlapping contradictions
to find a space your own: less than zero
or in over your head

The losers found their loss in the rough grounds
(Ronnie said)
denying what denies them
as if the whole emptiness
from mountain to shore
were a container for melancholy, like a fruit for juice

As if the zone of boundaries and measures
had an edge
and you could cross it
falling outwards into the dimensionless
the category of Space from which all real spaces devolve and distort
where Ideas became myth and edgeless sound
where all things are an exchange for all things

and the civic imagination reached the end of its figures
where indeed the future is whichever way you turn
fitting a curve to objectless light
and nothing to shelter you from the passing cry of geese
spectres at voluntary call

                      like phonons trapped in a crystal

(14)
The government falls from grace; Wigtown, 1685

The two offenders against the King's civil and religious state
by way of amendment
lashed to stakes on the foreshore
ranged one far up from the other
to drown at high tide
like mussels on a rock

The very stiffness of hemp
by air for the men, water for the women
The government holds itself divine, right,
innocent of their blood

as if the whole fetch of the ocean
from Newfoundland to Galloway
and the whole sweep of the moon
calling the ocean to shift its lair
were acolytes of the truth of Catholicism

as if the instances of the judiciary
or any other office soever
would have heard any opinion they had to say for themselves
except those which concerned their souls
and as such visitable with death

Margaret Wilson, aged eighteen years. Margaret MacLachlan,
          aged seventy.
contumacious mouths stopped with the Atlantic

Why have they forgotten the use of fire?
and why do they linger?
The purposeless tide rolls in slowly
but the swords of the Cameronians are later still.

The chancel of rain. The nave of bracken.
The Truth is wherever the law does not reach.
The Irish Sea spreads room for the defiant women
as if for fish within its silver dark
The idle sea takes back every step it takes forward
but the truthful do not forswear themselves

After these defections and judgments are over
ye may see
nettles grow out of the bedchambers
of noblemen and gentlemen

and
their names, memorials and posterity
to vanish from the earth

(15)
From the Book of Assassins; the reconstruction of the Crane Dance

Lying in the dark
wondering about the light
flicking off my face giving me away
cure the disease of knowledge

A leap through the window,
a race along the roof-ridge
pointed to and cried out
breathing through my soles
a flight from the chains of memory
Part the links of flesh. I caught their breath.

They set their dogs onto me
I was a scent at the core of my own death
a trail hot as a kitchen

The fugitive already captive
in fantasies with one end
voice and ego wasting away
I could feel my mind seeping out through my skin
to fill the room as a rare grey cube
An hour of bloody excess. Moonlight on a dulled blade.

A passage through darkness
where rays of light converge
on a lens of fright
I split them into two groups
and consumed them piecemeal

Inactivity and hallucination
the study of the assassin
the proper escort of their souls
they compassed wickedness and orated falsehood

From rags to marshes
the way through the sedge so long and turning
great clumps of roots stiff in the mud
the hulks of rotting boats green in the waterway
the home of drift and disuse
The water margins where nothing holds firm
and the map shows sleep and forgetfulness

To make a path of stooped and cracked willows
and gaze on herons at stance,
to lap cool green water from a ditch

I embroider waterfowl on a quilted jacket
trunks fallen headlong in pools and roots embracing air
stitching a rustling cloak of reeds
swim to the river island, pick the berries there
the octagonal red oak single-stick
the use of borage and watercress
saturated land and silted backwaters

To essay
the crane-dance
stalk and nod and turn
stiff-legged
on a lake margin
in the moonlight
dwelling on the swoop —
the plane of the mimic frog

three or four bloodstained purple stoles
the *via facti* or exoteric way

I practise archaic weapons forms
described in stiff strokes on clasps of bamboo-folios,
precious relics of forefather eras;
grotesque styles; courtly and rustic keys of movement,
the curves like those of a T'ang sacrificial bronze vessel

I spend the evenings imitating the call of birds
bright winged beetles settle on my garments

in the intermittence of reason
entire towns destroyed, ships sunk, hillsides collapsed.

Nomos, or Daily Forms

Space and nothingness foaming around our bodies
in three planes
where one is pigfast, slow, solidifies the earth, is steadfast
where one laps, outstretches, floats, ascends, swoops
where one runs down, intercepts, sweeps, matches
the body released into the command of the prime forms

meridians   swarms multiplicities
to the sound of expanding music
the edgeless space of the high wastes
drowning the equipment of State

the sequence of forms transforming all values
politics, metallurgy, and dance
the emptying of precious and laden objects
a glimpse of the loss and seizing of selves;
the sheets of parallel intensity
linking distant to near
like vast bands of solar light

the distant eye knows impulses decay,
the very ground is their ruins
so
we let the new peaks rush and swell us
slowed for a moment
searching for their way out

(16)

A stone tablet is found with Heaven's Commands in the Loyalty and Justice Hall; a plethora of Chinese wood-kemps on the old ran-dan

Hi, I'm Neil, and I'm your client adviser.
Mr Lu, I want you to explain to me
why you can't
take this job as a hypocrite and lickspittle
working for a Tory MP
at £3.10 an hour.

A still eye
within
the double centred vortex

Don't argue with me, I'll just recite the leaflet.
Here's an opening for someone young and without
prejudice
scraping muck off floors with a spatula
at £3.50 an hour
from 8 pm to 8am
conditions may be damp
must provide own protective clothing
employee is allowed to eat the scrapings

time is caught in the bright sequences
waveform strikes   sweeps, reaps, and throws
ripples across the unseen frame
a body thrown by weirs of energy in three planes
13 forms wait empty in the air

Neil pulled a vacancy on screen. Here you are,
rewriting Scottish history to remove the Scots from it

ability to deny all conscious agency a plus.
office environment. possibility of promotion.
no pay at first. If you turn an offer down
you may lose your benefit.

sketching the selective apprehension, we
skim above the unceasing flux of things
picking bands for their tinge or surface wear
with the finesse of the swordsman cultivating
the choices that compose consciousness itself
a pattern of a thousand unresolved strokes
maintained with an archaic rigour

What the security video catches is Neil as he
shore through the pillars with his Milanese sabre, leant back,
tossed an incendiary into the file store
and as the building fell to its knees
bowed to Lu Ta as his sifu.

(17)
Bodiless forms of the 'Internal Arts' Canon

The geosophical space-devising form

drawing out of the unperturbed emptiness
a Scottish mountain where deer flock in summer,
partaking of the image system of peaks, extremes,
ardent feats, far sight of the bard through sharp air
to the sea where galleys are sweeping;
home of intact virtue, shelter for outlaws and hermits;
where cairns mark the path though the snow is smooth;
where red burns boil in brief spate with crashing noise;
becomes a Chinese *tian*, where the intact
yang virtues of male ancestors topple in abundance,
where the clouds break to renew the dampness of the earth;
where a *tao shih* with skin like ice and snow
eats wind and dew and rides on cranes,
has light bones of the fabric called winter jade.

In time without features
we move through the rules of mental agility.
The form of reflexivity. Of aesthetic detachment.
Of dégagé sauntering through experience
of recognizing the eternal patterns of things
of accentuating what is delicate and exquisite
of deep fathomless attention on the original, ornate, and dazzling
the form of paradox, riddle, and mask
of figure-ground inversion, of switching perspective
of oscillation and ambiguity
of the vortex between double centres
of making convention conscious. Of breaking convention.
of hiding great strength beneath airy ornament
of lightly switching into two patterns at once

contrast and reverse. Foil and mirror.
Of dialectic and suspension. The form with several speaking parts.

Fighting off distraction and obscurity
glimpsing the *ching* of formlessness;
waking a hundred eyes of deep mindfulness
with a hundred kinds of unfamiliar shape;
commanding the learnt forms and the snap of an improvisation

(18)

Norval receives his martial instruction from the Hermit of the Grampian Cave; Lailoken takes to the forests to get over 'a personally bad time'

After three days' travel through the lands burnt by the English
at dawn they reached the beach by Castle Sweeny
where Himself was in residence, at oversight
of the vintage — dense ranks of ancient wine-presses
driven by spiral iron shafts with grapes as knobs
crushing the gush out of thick, ripe, splashing, purple bunches
which wooden tuns with yard-wide grins could hardly swallow
While the malting of Sweeny's barley
covered the sea with warm and sprightly fumes

And the gallowglass prince entertained them
in his snug hall entirely of red yew boards
frequently reciting from a vellum script in silver ink
tales called *Cogadh Suibhne,*
The Ranter's Foray, Sweeny furioso,
Strange Tales of Barry at the White Tiger Studio,
Outstanding Quagmire Tactics of the Redshanks,
and *Metrical Errors of Blind Arthur MacGurkich.*

A bit of an old Celtic relic
limestone foundations worn by sea-salt
but wearing his face with pride
that long handsome gentle dandy.

Fire and glass, in ample supply,
stripped the barley brew of its dark husks,
there dripped in overlapping furls
a pale supple rainlike run of strength

And so the heroes rested.

Visualizing Corporate Structure

A hole in a three-dimensional surface
pinpoints a gap in perception: light falls
on a missing plane.

We took the Minister of Selective Listening
round a park
of shattered businesses with red circles to mark
the weak point that wasn't in the model.
A shop full of sea-shells decks out
the plenitude and panoply of curves and hollows,
equations for a surface developed by spin
growing tenuous as it realises itself, each
a glimpse of the fertile unfailing allness
— radial, spiral, spherical, bivalve,
chambered, armoured, mottled, decussate —
surfaces for expressing process.
He understood the neck of a bottle.
Pointed cylinder with panels of chestnut and cream
distributed and separated.
Periodic spikes jutting from the test that frustrate
the staving clutch of the starfish, or, murication.

What are you visualising now?
the act of wandering round the building
wondering how to get the system across to my new boss.
Well, *this* is the coil winding shop.

Rooms of doctrine where the sets of actions,
the *Khrien*, wait to enact their transformations:
one files down a casting, one tests a circuit board
minimal units you
repeat or insert.

Group imperatives rolling across the building
speaking through a shared matrix
that can't be seen or written down.
Packing, arrays, phases, pores.
Precise voids. Domains. Casts of vesicles.
Robust solid foams. Aggregates. Agents
that copy themselves.
The squirting out of a globe-raft of eggs.
Telltales give what is silent a voice.

A rule of domination, possession, and expansion
viewing anything undepleted as its intake
A grab that takes the motherly soil
from its resting plane to the portal teeth
of whatever mills and tanks strip it of ambiguity,
volatilise fixed natures, to fix
the volatile. The asphradium,
a flapping organ dotted with chemoreceptors
acting as the barrier between in and out.

Moments where the invention of the register, the file, and the
          barchart
fishes up numbers and wipes
blood and scales off its fingers.
How many cubes of water in a net? Partitions
that keep ideas from washing away.
Graphics programmers tasked
to make the abstract
transparent, writing code for
drafting engines with a registration of 0.25mm.

The torsion of the developing body mass
to thread itself into the spiral shell;
asymmetry of organs for packing;
a pencil drawing a volute
with a jet of calcite crystals.

In the place of abundance
excess rolling our footfall

we feel faint as the pears block the road,
shoulders driving a shovel to find a way;
speaking faintly heard across the yards of goods
bury a mile of cloth beneath the overflow

An exponent of less than one
tracking an annual loss of substance
like the scrolls of a negative pitch:
where shattering looks much like origin
any shell is in your hand
because its inmate is dead.

The marks at the edge of the green resin backing
where it was sawed, part translucent
before any copper geography;
the paper tapes of movement programs
for the automatic board assemblers.
Where symbols drift on and off forms
a set of shared objects draw down the unknown.
Shared metaphors
make for successful conversations.

The brilliant collapsing of n dimensions
onto n minus 2; parallel ripples of pigment out
along a curving shell.
A mantle of bathing fluid called conchiolin,
a protein matrix where new tissue forms.

In a tall building there are so many damaged ideas.
A mesh with a running flaw that feels like perfection
Fails to wrap the invisible n-dimensional object
On whose surface your chances roll.
The management graphic
is not the shared symbolic model
which is not the true map
of the landscape and its fortunes.
Strategies of malacologists
for talking about the ideal mollusc.

Patterns competing for the same data
deposit passive arrays, sprawling.
Anomalies of shadow on a conjecture
contain the track of something unnamed,
clusters of events at its edges and foci
draw a minimal anatomy.
The true shape spread over many planes.
The tremor at the tip.
A tray
of exotica from the gaps between frame edges.

On some photographs taken at Government Criminal Camp Perm no. 35, in June 1989

Pachomius, in Lower Egypt
Led the way to the new life,
Breaking in the waste land,
Writing law in the desert,
Praying and fasting to kill the demons.
His hermits withdraw into the wilds.
Stephen of Perm went out into the North,
To the plains by the White Sea far
From the places where men gather, where
The senses are filled with confusion and error;
Deceit
A quality associated with humans.
Send the sorrowful out to clear the forests,
To repent and contemplate when the senses are emptied.

When they lock you in the unheated cell, in winter,
The cold nipping at your skin,
Numbing hands and feet, gradually
Drains the head of ideas, to make way
For awareness of objective needs.
As reactionary errors weaken
The proofs of Materialism take on a pristine glow.
The reformatory value is clear;
As your fingernails turn blue you can check
That reality is as the community leader says.

A race whose faces all look the same:
Fat reserves missing, curves
Shrunken to straight lines, profiles
Drawn and hard like insect heads.
The spiritual blue tinge

Of a penance,
Hunger concentrating the spirit to repent
Its sins and vagaries
Against the lord who brings the food.

Ghost Technology, part 2: The Extreme Computing Fair, or the Festival of Inappropriate Technology, 9.6.02

Cognition! Ignition!
the diet sheet for a selfish intelligence
whose goal is to be acquired by an environment
destabilising at speed
which falls asleep if it slows down, so
has to build a region of risk, predictably
unpredictable & soluble
the shaped charge of data
in slow pleasurable struggles
voracious of its own distortions
I mean, like 500 extremist computing buffs
colliding in a municipal hall in Camden
an off the radar cyber jumblesale
their powdery green spores of data
self-recoding as they
spread over ideas
like mould over a bag of apricots

The idea as pleasure
the stand up solid buzz you get off it
the neural assimilation time stretched
– cognitive frames bouncing –
till comedown time *score some more*
whole-body cerebral response
verbal combat to mutually impress
the keepers of prestige *let's do it again*

I was measuring energy flows
in machines that had stopped working
a skyscraper of which one floor is a big glass

tank, full of reptile brains staying up late.
territory & aggression & comparison of body parts
sharp colours of the limbic landscape,
bright cool water to play in,
basking beach with louvre windows slatted for
the serotonin gushes, the flavours of perfect magenta,
the biocosmic highs: pineal overload
preparing the archaic returns of culture, the
Apollonian games. The arcade of the sun.
innovations brought about by warfare

brains wiped to frame impingent light
data lizards with strained eyelids
& unrepaired skin, nights lost in the fuzz
seeing whole galaxies on infra-red
turning white noise into new kernels
frazzled retinas as membranes
staring to the edge of the universe!

we shared our vision with the suits and they left the building
a permeable membrane with one side on the cosmos
environment as organ trays of new milled lenses
or, perception as competitive collecting
where storing the max number of past states
is winning
gain a whole new shopping identity!
mint film
of optical scans
tearoffs stored or simulated
the rare interstitial objects grabbed and saved
sorry — had that experience before!

We are trudging through the 1950s
down the back streets of that grimy Northern town
to where the mil-surplus shop with its piece parts of the Cold War
has decked out its trays of lenses and prisms
to lure pre-teens sifting and sighing in a basement.
Swept by the course of light

I wanted to take it home.
For spiral starlight recessed snares
the shed organs of great aircraft
dwellers in the drowning skies of the North Atlantic
fingers feeling for shore, star or beacon
appeasing their appetite for great space.

We were accelerated to a horizon
adapting sight in the workshop of telescopes
a refined art whose only end is transparency
 to mutate the world-building software behind it.
Stripped and reworked fossils of machines to come
repurposed & *ex situ*;
spying on the sexuality of stars
in the abyss of light we constrain the invisible.
Glass eyes glinting on the beach of starlight, you don't know
how little the bosses of 1959
know about an engineering civilisation!

It's not a game
unless you can start from zero
with no status and no alliances
and lose to someone faster
the red-eyed raiders into a desert space
debris scattering prismatic dust
into hidden corners
all trajectories vectors
reflectors to a burnt eye
freestyle dust in the lurches of cognition
where we use words like *teeming* and *spawn*
to show something acephalous and bursting our
small movement tracking codes
what do you do at the margin
where comprehension ends?
not all at once
receding in a dapple with a clock pulse

Large scale behaviour of engineering firms
latched onto contest games of young engineers

the mill of data-greedy bodies
like a scorpions' mating beach
deception and imitation
I want to try it
Young incomplete aggressive programs
ageing into melody & satiation
confusing a simple R/C timer
and a ceramic resonator clock!
By the Extreme gaming stand
where there was a hole in the graph
there was a hole in the behaviour

Making up games to avoid boredom
inversion/deletion things
that become a new mathematics
that everyone plays
tacit rules of shifts and constants
made audible by
the blurred quadrant and its unfaithful program
that idly hashes thru the stored sequences
idiot CHOP and CONCATENATE *wanna play?*
Once you store national culture you *know*
it's going to be transcoded
a set of symbolic sequences
locked to repeat themselves: JUMP TO HEAD
where *eternal* of course means repetitive
where *national*
means "writing copies of themselves"

A floor littered with serial tryouts
if it *worked*, it wouldn't be leading edge
a roomful of traumatised kit.
slighted loves. distorted by acts of love.
cut and strapped. gashed. wires bared,
wrenched into new specs.

the monster garage. the Burgess Shale of electronics
fighting over new organs
dead until the last minute

fascias unsmoothed by designers
unshielded. Changing every day.
cuts and straps like a butchered bat
softening the hardware
mutant battlefield equipment
for storing egos in
that still want to play
still want to stay up later
have you got those Red Galaxy videos?
weeks of nailing trivial bugs
pounding round the same track
till the loop breaks: the
terrestrial edge
where paladins dismount to seize
an unheard-of pattern

No Joshua Logan
Colours of dawn over the East Pacific.
Barge-fired off-beach
nuclear device "Greenhouse Dog" puts on a big show
for Ted Taylor who 15 miles away
straps on goggles no 3D at count -30.
The Martini glasses
above the beach house bar
chinked filled with shockwave,
overbrimmed —
and cracked in two

Swimming in Spirals

Searching patterns in the Out, missing the attractor waves

there in the sea of gravity
we heaved ourselves upright in our shackles
fire-canisters threw us out
onto the broad strand

The harness fell off our motions
days of improvised and elaborate gesture
days of effacing borders
every thought traced out
in the heated tank with its forest of weeds
fluent through the linked waterways
in colours of blue and red

Flitting through our own space
flickering in green flare-dappled shadows
& dance in rings among our echoing wet images
patterns glancing out of our spines

I thrash like a tunnyfish
I swish like a reptile
I tumble end over end

The dynamic body ripples a record
on the flat white surface primed for roil prints
The spin of the newts in their tank alerts the pilot
seconds before the drag catches and spins the ship

The ship's planned course (each celestial mass
is a motor, like the ship's; where mass hides without light
and the fine stones in the ear shift to relate the ego to

the verticals local to each centre of Down)
is printed on the screen
where the swimmers' arms left their movements

Weightless in the muscular web
for months until the spiral stabilizes.
Exact radii. Sheaved loops. Among us.
The natives of red water see shapes flow out of their wrists.

In the Echo Nebula
tides shift
as the swimmers' bodies
with a lead of hours
turbulent matter sealed
with the signature of neural patterns, bursts
scoring the white stones cast up on the shore

external bodies litter the Unconfined,
swim into the coves of space

Echoing each others' movements
in the connected shallow pools flowing as air with sound
where clouds of warmth drain us of frustration
the reptile body steals over the laxed primates
the momentary universe of discourse
reconfigures the artificial lake

Blauer Reiter at Ducketts Common

In the blond pine bookcase to the left of the door
The Thames and Hudson book with the photograph
Of the hanging in felt appliqué, with the
Rider in blue tunic and yellow hose
In straight eyelines with the Mother Goddess in full insignia
Repeated all around the wall
Of the ice-lined tomb at Pazyryk, 5th century BC,
Tumbles in the world of the flat, strict profile, and colour patches

And ten feet away on the green chair at the table
With the dead plants and the landlady's hurricane lamp,
In the clothes of a 17th C Greek aristocrat,
Karagöz, the Hero Puppet painted on leather
On a poster for a Turkish festival I tore off the wall by Ducketts
    Common,
Joins up with the Rider: a line that followed the Turks
From the Altai mountains to the Mediterranean vines.
There Karagöz in his boat hat, his green breeches and yellow
    stockings,
His red riding-tunic whose skirts fall almost to the knee,
Its white appliqué flowers and lace jabot,
Fights for the Faith without shifting from the flat plane.

Memory is pressed into a new frame
And matched for fit, two years of
Gawp era, lummox conduct are over. I was so excited
I could barely stand, clogged faculties uttering

To hot-wire the connection which Luci said wasn't there.
What resemblance? Wasn't I proud
To know my sentimentality about folk art,
My weakness for anything Turkish and Inner Asian,

My credulity about traverse cracks in the fabric
Had come back?
I can talk again even if I'm not telling the truth.

She wears a full-length dress *juste au corps* and a big pillbox hat
          with jags,
He has a moustache and a little leopard-skin cape stiff out on
          the wind,
A band of brocade divides his body exactly in two,
She sits on a throne, has our crown-tines, and holds the Tree of Life.
If I write the dialogue that's spurious too.

Do you think I could buy those clothes
Somewhere between Turnpike Lane ABC and the New River?

Rhythmic Blind Spot

Scorpion
                    in the mongoose's shadow
Step counter step
                    in symmetry of parrying
With the lethal prick
                    drawn to the hunter's music
In one more pattern
                    than the poisoner knows
A swing-shift
                    of captivating allure.

After the hard, the soft. Before the bitter, the sweet.
From ardent to cool.
The thief, the hunter, and the artist
Mock what they study most
And fill what knows them
To defect from it.

 This moving cube of light
                where the soul is caught
                        eats light and moves to find stillness.
A drama with no outside, both true and false
improvised by two just one syllable at a time.

In the full compliance and locking-to
A white space opens
Plain and lost to sight.
A new height at which you're frozen
in a pose of base strain
is a clear pipe for the new sound to flow down.

Because she's more intelligent than you
A white space emerges in the music
You pleased what you predicted
And what else cut you down.

Andy-the-German Servant of Two Masters

The right family connections
and an edited biography. Deep cover
and a foreseen shortage of infantry wars. Theorist
of stalking. Long-range shooting
is mainly
a spiritual thing

The first thing you do, you get them
to buy automatic weapons
This breaks the ice and makes their fingers tingle.
One hand on the bottle and one…

Andy, Mr *Bundesverfassungsschutz* is not Budweiser,
Talked as much as someone with a mouthful of water.
That is, he swallowed the words and passed the water out as
            social gifts
How much can a building really take?

ritsch, ratsch
hang out the trash. The jury will buy
a limited hang-out. America for the Americans
Shine for the shoeshine boys
Land for the lords. Sacks for the shucks.
Elohim City for Oklahoma.
Draff for the hogs. Fish for the seals.
A bag for the sleaze. A bowl for the dust.

Time for crime. Day for night. Green for red.
Beyond the beaming tautologies, everything
profound loves a mask, and
people with dirty souls
don't wear swoop necklines.

The ATF guys weren't in the office that day
the office blew out of the building
Blew the town. No-showed their showdown.
Blow the gaff. Cut the smoke
in the open-plan with its façade cut away
to foreclose the government. Blow it out your ears.

Ozarks-scale gene pool bi-bi-bitten by a gun bug
Doorstep Andy selling a script
like throwing sticks for a dog.

Way down
way over where the steel rods breach
where the steel pins break-dance
where the parked cookup cracks the theorised linear frame,
watch out! where the classic curve of a blast wave
met the tectonic cement cubes
at the imaginary point in geometry;
and a citizen's rights man
with a doctorate in the mathematic of ruin,
brass Air Force general with
big back-up in negative civil engineering says
no way
could McVeigh have torn their playhouse down
We control the horizontal
He heard a skip-beat in the wall of sound

we control the vertical.
The updating of moral consensus. The conduct
of the gaze. Altering shared ideas
by cover of night. Sending to fantasies.
Threads run out as clues
adding grey noise to data excess
in a screen with key escrow. Where sight lines converge,
pinned against the horizon, a thief sideways
behind your back. How come the musicians know
what's coming next? From shoo-in to death-watch,
spinning data back through a false third party.

Hiding pattern in pattern, breaking outlines,
snap-point shear from appliquéd charges on the pillars.

I'm gonna run to the City of Refuge,
turn about, hire a captain of the watch
with the skills of a career infantry officer,
crossing the Great Plains without breaking a contour line.
The oculist of blind spots just walked in through the in door.
Fully automatics for the camp guards.
Elohim City Compound
is the outside of the inside.

Andy two for one. Andy fluent in the manly skills,
draw them in over the head handy.
The barrels are beautifully rifled and the marksmen
are destabilised, we figure
someone who believes what we believe
is too double dumb to double talk
a trick track where the phase of confined movement
flows on from conducted freedom of action.

Blow, Illinois, blow! the righteous highs
of homesteader holdouts, Indian killers
and Bible readers, stake racers
and redneck heads of household;
their gold,
                guns
                        and water
clinking on taut skin, tall-walkers
waving half a wit taught
civics by an
occupation government. Up-country
applejack and freeze-dried buffalo cocks.
Plenty too smart to eat soil.
Keepsakes from the Dolly Parton Theme Park,
Theologoumena in No Roads County.

A fervour of conjecture
where whatever fleshes out the fixed idea

is drawn in to draw on,
bent surface proteins as wrappers for
the end of the game. It was like selling
perimeter captains to paranoids.

While the verses give no light, living out of
the back of a truck, running with
a travelling gun fair, the country
flaring behind you like a contrail, from mesas
to trailer parks, wrapped up tight at
the vanishing point. The round jumps straight
and for a moment
your soul is held between your shoulder and forefinger.
The pamphlets go out with the home defense goods.
Sight line, white lines,
riding the hiss-hot rails to a place of Federal care.

Antelope headgear of a mimic
spear-carrier.
A verbal trail discarded by
military intelligence is
interference pattern:
leopard's spots against
tree foliage
blinking with sun.
Antique stalker skills bagging
a far political organisation.

One hand on the bottle and one . . .
Andy sitting out at night with a Midwest blonde.
Andy's square dancing drill squad pissing testosterone
Slapping heel and toe with the Hessian.
Steadily losing arguments with the Devil.
Rolling in the Surrey with the fringe on top
Andy knocking in stakes and lines in Strassmeir County,
Buying federally restricted rounds by FedEx.
Andy kickin' back. Andy digging Western Swing.
Andy fading up the patches of blur.
A lurk in the lurch. Damned straight, in the straddle.

Poems Unwritten, in Faint Exhaustion, One Sunday Night

Poem in the manner of JH Prynne
Poem in the manner of Brian Marley
Poem in the manner of Mark E Smith
Celtic ethnographical forgery poem with technophile cataracts

Poem suitable for recitation by Hockey Girls in pale yellow sweaters
Socialist Art deco poem with glass cylinders and aluminium tubes
Poem containing low-budget shopping
Poem containing high-budget shopping

Typological poem in isometric modules
Poem in the manner of Ralph Hawkins
Poem with linebreaks subtly displaced
Poem with linebreaks in between the lines

Poem in the manner of a Thuringian follower of Thomas Kling
Poem in the later manner of Karlien van den Beukel
Poem in the manner of Michael Ripper
Poem in the manner of Peter Mandelson

Poem displaying high-fashion ideas
Poem displaying High Street ideas
Poem displaying inner-circle ideas recognizable to the outer circle
Poem set in Loughborough

Poem containing sexy actress
Poem containing 2 sexy actresses
Poem containing depressed clerical and phone worker
Poem containing poet

Club Classics poem
Dance Drama with interpretative parts for Seven Scorpions
Poem without a list structure
Poem in the modern style

Poem made up of data + procedures
Psychedelic poem
Poem with a programme of modernization in government
Poem in which words alternate

The Dressmaker

Bubbles of sun
on lager and fine naked shoulders,
on a raft made of coarse earthenware, you
dive and surface in the beer, in a dizzying
backwater, where a dead carcass
slowly stains a pool rich with froth.
You gorge and vomit this,
oils draining out of your skin
to ease your heart.

Or tint a bare scene into the inauthentic.
As the dance swirls through the lower floors
the attendants in dark gloss fatigues
bake you in hops and butter,
pass you through the porcelain skylight
throw you off the building

You flare as you descend to applause,
Take the young man on your arm.
In a pavilion of twelve layers of materials
You shear and stitch a deep exterior, say
I control the impressions. I script the reactions.

Adjust a mismatch of outside and inside,
Dress in a green and white striped waistcoat,
perform a series of intricate and unrepeating steps,
find the young man gone. The barman
presses your face into black liquid.

The music is a sexual hymn
costumes filled by the wind
rush to embrace each other,

flirt, sulk, turn languor
from a slur into a flood of sound,
pair off in a shared gesture.

The crowd is sinister and dedicated,
peels starfish from the dish.
Exchanges tributes of prestige,
empties glass sleeves of chilled toxins.
Turn eyes every time the door opens,
tear favours off their companions,
their dear hearts.

The woman who fits every dress you stitch
in fabrics soft as water, bright as fruit
commands silence, action, trust, fights, tears, joy,
says and spoils everything you will say.
Lifts your finger. Distorts your face.

You go together through the bar full of
eyes floating on glass stems to
the back room where the disbanded companies
of assassins in their pale silks
dress you in ox leather and cut your arms off,
reveal you in fripperies and furbelows.
Complete a dance step. Photograph you.

Now that the river under your window
reflects a steady image, in a hundred slipping shards
each for a few seconds, at the standing of the
flow, at the gleaming of the effaced,
forgive me everything I saw, as
I forgive you everything I say.

On the planting of a new National Forest in Staffordshire and Leicestershire

Oak, ash, field maple, wild cherry,
lime, walnut, larch, Scots pine, Corsican pine.
Slight saplings held upright
as county councillors stoop to safeguard
the helpless wands, stood in muck, the solicitude
draughted to cover the wrecked lands in new forest
flowing to reach the old stands of Needwood and Charnwood.

Gleams in the glass of furnace slag
eloquence inked in the rich soot of clinker
topsoil seared with a torpid blade
of toxic metals
lash of chimney plumes laden with particles
black rains
dropping their high-temperature loads with a sigh.

Fleet of trees in launch of shafts of sap
metabolic glow to heal a sick land
green tops rising from darkened root
where the waste of manufacturing
mixed poisons with the surface of the earth.
The city of dead substances
the ranges of spoil tips
sterile, without bacteria
the landscape of strip mines
neither living nor dead

It looks
like a projection of hatred
it feels
like the allegory of a sick body

a distortion of the inner organs
high-temperature sealed layer
without thermal exchange
the trees inserted like reaction vessels
where pools of waste water had long stood
and spoil heaps washed out traces that killed streams
to nurture and heal the poisons.

Once
where a tall straight tree had grown in Saxon groves
it took a family out to sea
light hull clenched with wooden nails
woven like the walls of a house
laded, launched in the sea-creek
slipping into grey sea-horses, billows,
steering out past Heligoland, Zeeland, Dogger
with the thickness of a board
between them and the all-devouring sighing sea.
Star rise, blood crossed naked
light hulls stowed with seed
where birth is near oblivion, a human group
tumbling out onto a strange shore.
As the land wakes from its sea, a new home heaves in sight,
silver rivermouths asking for the hull.
The fields of Nene the tribes of Trent
the floodbed of Avon the shores of Soar
Popped out from wooden shell.

The forest survived on the ridges; Needwood, Charnwood, hursts
Looking out at each other across human fields.

Extents of Charnwood
where a mighty tree fallen
leaves a hollow by its roots
filled with red water
against pale clay

where the pile of fallen leaves
is warm to the touch

where the sharp sound of winter streams
rattles over stones

Cycles for the reversal of time
features vanishing in blanking process
organs dissolving in a liminal flow
the earth losing its memory
to return to an eternal Now
new land growing under the forest
like what the glaciers ploughed up and washed out
where personality is lost where sound is lost
where damage is buried and crossed

Mainadik scholia

the lifting of the knee the turning of the ankle
the arcing from the waist the foot in mid-air
all defining what lies between the legs

the burning of flesh framing forests in the escaping light
seeing everything only at speed
limbs flinging wide as energy flows upwards and out
heated light flashing off white skin
flame puffed up with blast of air
the world one great heat-haze
flickering and rolling

the recoiling phrase
where the cataract that cuts its line into the mountain
and makes its steady roar in passage
breaks up on upthrust stones
the uneven energy
of the exalted dance
that breaks its own measure

oreibasia
through daring, ardour, self-excelling
a dithyramb
that never drops its dancers to earth
never repeats itself
and never runs out

on the mountain where there are no crops and no property marks
no laws and no buildings no status and no account of time
where there are rhythms but no words
eis oros eis oros

a grouping released in marble
a whorl still around its centre
limbs laxed from heroic discharges
arms gravely embracing sleep

The Very First House

The fourth rightangle that was turned
wholly demarcated inside from out
a kind of clay bowl, blown up with a breath of air,
containing the first home

Opening the door a peek, you heard
Strains of voices speaking, sobbing, telling.
The sounds filled the room with a comforting presence.

Without direction,
one went into the sitting room with the port, purple and mulberry,
one went to wander through the forest near the house,
one went into the scullery and plunged her hands into greasy water.

As play, to start with, you imitated those voices
Until you could make up the next pages of script for yourselves.
Breaking the silence which left body and objects in close balance
Which now seemed rustic and dull.
You closed the door and the words stopped.
In each room you did what the voices said
Becoming carried away, hearing one voice you shut the others out.

They found ideals, shapes cut in crystal to whose
Plan they stretched and dressed and spited their own limbs,
Febrile without outline, like gleaming vapour.
Alterated, in penance and sacrifice
They found distorted images of themselves
Loved and transgressing. The first family.

Every house has some things that no-one knows how to use.
It was never possible to grow fur for warmth or messages,
But piles of clothes were folded neatly in the drawers.

No indication of how to wear them,
How to match them up, who was authorized
After what trials, to put them on.
Procedures had to be invented.

Ambient forces had to be snared.
Three warm containers: the air inside, the body, the pot.
Three places of chemical change: the stomach and limbs, the
        pot again, the mould growing green on the white bread.
Three sites of moisture: mouth, eaves, kitchen wall where
condensation chills out. Three protective barriers.

Linen grew in the fields around, it turned out
To be for cricket bat oil, old wood,
A black crunchy bread, whites next to your skin,
For writing annals on, string, and sails.
Its organs were part of the lived material layer.

A cooking pot the exact same shape as the house
each with hollow space and skin,
both locking moisture and heat,
but fired for different times.

On the first table
there were envelopes with instructions.
Distinguish between clothes and blankets
Let light in, keep water out
Don't make hats out of pottery
Don't eat mice. Don't kill spiders.

"Wear hampering clothes. Gossip and wheedle.
Strive to please. Strike with the flat hand.
Tend poultry."

"End discussions by firm assertions.
Use horses and metal. Work out in the field."

"Accept the signal to invert it.
Occupy whatever goes against A.

Whatever he is good at is bad.
You don't need his food and water. Never give way.
Nag away for years until you have forgotten whatever A knows, until
you can't see anything he sees.
Black out parts of your eye. This means you're brothers."

When the curtains were closed
The walls flickered with images with no light source.
They watched film of the future occupants
In between the set pieces they had to make most of it up,
Gawping for awkward minutes while they tried to find a cue.
repeating sentences until a context for them turned up.

*"Gnaw bread left uncovered. Memorize paths through big space. Run
along grassblades to reach the seeds. Build nests out of paper and
wisps of linen, with granary. Fight for territory. Leave streaks of piss
everywhere."*

Self-reproducing Programs, Property Regimes

The most beautiful verbal space of a world
where I lived peacefully like an animal
that I damaged when I started to act
in repetitive fragments
in the belief about my brother
that what was his wasn't mine,
barraging into his every sentence
damaging the shared space of listening
seeking something new that I could say.
Wanting to be alone with the love I stole
where is the bit that belongs to me?
in Loughborough, in 1960. in 1963

Social structure is nothing but
the urge to repeat.
the imperative whose start I didn't know and don't.
I forgot it because my parents disliked it,
a piece of monster code that crept into the main sequence.
The recurrence of sequences is not yet melody.
A mouth cloyed by what it learns
and an eye eaten by what it sees
a screen detecting & imaging disaster
a liquid which is exchange for all things
enveloping its objects in sensitive film

An appetite switched on by pattern
ignoring every sector except its own
narrowing spectrum to maximise
repetition of its chosen sequence
and gorge who knows what pining cell.
Colours that swell and slack to show
bacteria fighting on a dish,

little machines that knock out their song and stop;
the patches of colour repeating outwards to cover
the visible plane of Leicestershire.
Cycling of tense and slack
an unstable nucleus whose structural flaws
cause a population of oscillations in surface
allowing choice at a later date
a soft acquirer destabilised by its own actions

The younger brother jealous of the smaller gift,
the simpler toy, breaches west,
into an empty matrix where the second
shall be first, into a zone of fictive signs,
copied and mutated strands,
where new teritory can be ejected for no cost

                                        Full but not satiated
A bird taught by an array of cloths and mirrors
sharp eye accustomed to repeat
coming down from 1500 feet to the niche
the reconnaissance enough for safe return.
a milieu defined by memory
an acoustic dazzle in a shell shape
outlining the body plane
a shimmer of reference beams, evanescent flux lines
recursively self-correcting:
a coping that wants its way
drinks up & recodes other patterns.
From brothers fighting
acquiring inner conflict. What I swallowed
may be the office of younger brotherhood.
He's a tax lawyer and I just talk a lot.
I did a mediaeval degree, bardic and barbaric,
he used to work in the *ducal department*
— well, somebody has to own the country.
The law projects power beyond personal death
& holds the drifting scuds of the land together.

Voices as masks, masked voices
Buried circular resources that spend
and empty
and turn. Dramas of kinship; learning of lines.
Control dispersed to several hundred
closed programs running, away from sight.
A mouth
allowing signature to emerge? or recording scenes?
A program of vacuity
seizing sequences of code in mimetic greed
repeating them to acquire parts of a voice
rich in barbaric assimilations
seized by its beautiful captives
a deposit of inversions and repetitions
steeped in minerals of biological deposit
the compiled suite of gaudy origins
bathed in gold-drenched fluids
populated with surface-filling curves.
It rolls to a head and turns to repeat

Precipice of Niches

1.
the latest wish of
a data fish
that eats and becomes an ego
that swallows and is hungry again

a mineral ego
grinding the beds of earth for pigments
of grey and blue
soaking into the colours of the landscape
fading between drab and opaque
the curve where its mouth closes
dispersing over the bed of the visible
to swallow itself at the horizon line

soft as an eye and fresh as air
the droppy deity of sweet water
that falls everywhere
and uses the sky as its path

naked in flash floods
a niche fish that knows in flashes
that adopts the colour of the air
and recites the tale as told it

the casing of volatile sound

a niche fish flushed with signs
that worships the living waters above the dead

2.

The coast was called Moors in Hell
its rocks lurched in twisted planes
where a cliff had slipped its step and top-
pled, split and split again
to become the seabed;
ruin as complexity, interior swallowing each surface,
riddled, a perfect refuge for what hides
and haunt for what catches
a geometry of fine-scale degradation
in its traps and part-worlds

The viewing-glass viewed
the pored littoral paradise
scattered over many acres,
in frames, in niches
its bursts and splashes of rock,
surfaces glinting red green and tawny
scored with blind signs, gripped by shells,
each pit fitting
the strange anatomies of the deep.

3.
The eye that sheds grains of dust

The hypothesis
of the X-wind
the flux double-peak, the X-zone
where a star's metals splash out & escape
like water that leaves the sea,
and a flake away where a lash of the Sun's magnetic field,
moving in, slung matter out from its outer edge
spume dense enough to aggregate
on an orbit where growth & cooling were possible:
the spores of a planet

The tidemark
a phase trapped in chondrule insets, in

falls of Libya and Antarctica
meteorite eye protected by stone
whose ball retains the archaeology of a vapour
aluminium isotopes marking a boiling point,
heavy nuclei a solar origin

slender birth line of a planet
solution to a kinetic geometry
marginal to so many dead states
slowed on a slope of dispersal & destruction
becomes its own environment, an I-scene
cascade of self-speeding attractiveness
trapping indifferent volleys of impacts

the twin of dead twins
of isotopes vaporizing into derelict wastes,
that uniquely peaks with the recurring turning-back,
the self-storing spores

4.
A passive and incomprehensible surface
a culture leaving its Time in puzzles and masks
wonderful & unfamiliar self, a perfect refuge
growing and dividing at visible speed
tremulous in many leaves dancing,
in vaults where the deep dark forms sift and sop around
recreating shells of lost moments
where horizons part and deny each other
a foam of local ends to vision
a matrix shimmering with traps and part-worlds

Short-lived selves discolouring in a decay cycle
a shell of evanescent subsonic waves
in the field recordings of ritual music
the square scripts of the southern oases
recording the high death of ibexes
solution to a kinetic geometry

for the replenishment of the high springs
eyes of water where unknown wishes surface

as we swallow the rich and alien forms
a fan of dialects & early inscriptions falling
down a slope of broken symmetries
we ascend to match the past
spreading in a strained and saturated web
sets dense in doubles & contrasts form
a screen allowing us to ignore all sounds

passing into temporary bodies
linked to capes of sensation
craving for rare metals, the slopes of old
rock stiff with solar riches
pursuing the slender birth line of birds
to the Western shores
wings sheathed in the fossil matrix
a complex made serial
and anatomy formed in myth
recurring time
where the darkness opens its eyes to us
its rare phonemes & brilliant plant dyes

Photographing the Ideal

A hall of people
Swimming in soft darkness, acquiescent
In a spiral of light drawing upwards
To a memory they don't own

We spend the afternoon asking the ash tree to look like itself
The rich browns and greens
Adorning the skin of a shared symbolism
The painterly idea caught on camera in 1942.
The sight which immerses and satisfies
demonstrating human scale to a horizon of low hills.
A stand of old growth beech and ash
beside a river running through green meadows
at a depth to which we consent
not caring from where the river refills,

apparently it slopes back to replenish itself.
Queer that what feels like Eden looks
so poor when filmed from the wrong spot

Fog of tree pollen caught by contrast with the sky
shaking, for an instant before invisibility
spill of life lured out by mildness of air
beaten by the sun like dust from a flour-bag
a million entire fragments crouched on the wind

A swarm of small desires that soars
trailing scarves of light, dying satisfied.
Those Shell posters looming as a colour key.
Beddington's spec for the landscape sequences

was strict — matching his other films,
England the brand. On every tin.

The small raddled window of the cinema reel
instructing a thousand towns in what they know

The delicate senses overflowed
with green excesses. Head gone to ground.
Going nowhere. There. A lens marked with
concentric versions of how the self fits into space,
vanishing in spectral blur at the horizon line.

I photographed the young woman in the river,
asked her for a date in the pub up in the village
not on: talking about white flesh against green barley
not on: talking abut the spectrum gaps in panchrome stock

Shots planned by Victor from Occupied Europe.
A flush of hormones affecting my colour sense
a nuptial wind inflamed by the forests of the past
undetained by the heaviness of the sunset
abandoned to flight without knowledge

Vertical Features Made Out

Flying at 1000 feet to shoot a film magazine
wings level to secure the match-ups,
making serial scans as flat as sized paper,
dreaming of tracing heat and moisture,
shooting air instead of ground.
Clean and sweet unresisted
swoops from horizon
to horizon of the earth
shouldering all kinds of wear.
Down, on a looted table with back-lighting
exposures with overlaps sanded and glued,
a patience that shows how space joins to itself.

Allover soft skin feeling of the green beloved earth.
Rivers in summer reduction crimped to ideal curves.
Subjectivity washing over the returns of light
like winged insects too fine for the lens to resolve
like haze or swallows.
Top-head-on pinpoint sharp
reduced to the head of a pin,
a whole gulp of depleted recognition.
Recovered by looking,
an aerial world forced back into terrestrial language.
Headstocks lost in foreshortening given
back by the detail in their shadows.

Parallel flight of a starling, in its month, from the sea,
sailing its eye over blocks of territory
the signs of the good land caught, as seen:
visual rhyme with a new home
& I could be happy here
— the signal to dive into the expanding picture.

Suspended in the long scans of exposure
snatched up in the view the rain sees
walking the beams of air and light
Sweeps at right angles to line of flight
reveal the extents of what was fantasized
chain of halation along watercourses
vertical features made out.
The sheer scale
picking out structure in the subsoil,
anatomy raising a colour contrast

where light falls straight and glare
is read-back as reflexivity of smooth surfaces.
A pyramid of earth reveals itself in the direction of flight
the lost site's
relief sharp in the stereoscopic lenses
looming through ground cover emaciated by heat.
A giant structure, an anomaly of the countryside
surfacing through a dark sea,
last recorded in the 13th C
& a speckled blur might be a flock of birds.

The horizon tells us what we are
visual cues recalling sets of actions
a dome filled and emptied by light.
Hanging over the desired land
losing scale in the footloose sky,
losing zone to plunge back through time.

The Star Temple of Sumatar Harabesi

From the staining of woven linen or plaster
with pigments or dye, suited to spreading or soaking
boundaries freeing a space
where the invisible becomes visible
it opens for us to enter the revealed world.
To begin with the motion of time
an air heavy enough
that we fall slowly
the opening of a bowl of space
where figures are distributed
enveloping multiple still
blue air behind which wider light is hidden,
passes

The scheme of influence comes from the head of the Tigris
as the book *Picatrix* with its decans,
the patches of total influence
colouring whoever is shaped and born,
thirty-six covering the whole rim of the year.
Man with dark complexion and red eyes,
wound in white cloth, angry, raising a two-leafed axe:
one of the prosopa,
faces for the entire
field of astral forces
brighter than sound
and more rational than light.
Latin version of an Arabic book:
from Harran in Syria, the citadel of the moon-worshippers

And their star temple in the hills, quite near:
Sumatar Harabesi. Seven buildings
of seven signed ground-plans
each with a vault beneath, the grotto

for births, the cistern soaked by the planetary,
The isolation from the healing influence
the fasting from all that is lovely
the darkness burst by starlight
and the rebirth into creative supernal light.
The laws of the stars
laid out in a magical doorless room in the Romagna
triplice strisciata pittorica
emerging from the dark conch into brightness.
The palace at Schifanoia
rezoned as tobacco factory.
The re-opener
swept pigment off the floor
firm external space, its generous lap
poured in a heap. Five months missing,
scraped off with the whitewash in 1820,
reduced to pure colour volume, a shower in flakes.
The rest — the decans with their proper objects
running around the walls of a *salone*, no start,
the year's ring and the cycle of human possibilities.
Volume-creating pigment uttering
a wave theory of the universe,
A planet covered in patterns
like scoops and ripples on the surface of water.
Rays filling the interorbital spaces like sound
whose scrolls lap over a planet
falling spirally, with the noise *rhoizos*
to expend themselves in substance.
Print an image in a spray of spinning drops;
water held in a swirl by twin attractors
stands for the trapping of subtle energy
into the cell whose fluids
cluster round the origin of form.

The milled thing
that traps light in flat truth
patches of shading grain according to grain
unthinking metal tube that sees
but has nothing like Sight

Can you see your ideas? what do they look like?
how would you fit England into a picture? or,
how would you visualise happiness? in the grouping of human
        beings?
So many volumes to show in history
the fulfilment of a schema.
The ideal is built up gradually
from attempted moments of sharing
stabilised by a kind of exhaustion
where violent impulses reached serenity
the shell of an idea
as a struck string finds sound retrieving it
stored safely within call.
In this magical room the states of Time
are caught like colour on a white screen,
the pleasures of the court, the work of the peasants,
the thirty-six Star Demons
whose energies are resolved in human actors.

Search spiral through the signs and the featureless
The court accepts the disclosures.
The end of all motion when the eye is
calmed by what it wanted to see.
Centres of happiness that draw events around them?
careful re-enactment of the central scene?
Play that gradually comes to seem like life?
sets of tryouts that unstoppably converge?

A window where we enter the shaped world
to try out the movements of time
an air heavy enough
that we fall slowly into temporal form.

The Whole History of Heresy

(1) *A Minor Tradition*
the defeated party walking into silence
shattered in the courts of the State
vaporised in derelict hill ranges
hiding in villages, burning their writings
teaching great heresies face to face
parallel traditions on the margins of court culture
parodying its provincial copies
altering codes, Gnostic theology in the hill dialects,
the naming of the sound of the stars
the cultivation of saffron for its dust

(2) *Alexander Peden*
The hundreds of armed men set to kill an idea
drove the Word out of Galloway

With firelocks to release bodies from their souls
from a cave in a brae in Ayrshire, living,
a small heat glowing in rain and darkness
Peden crossed the border in secrecy.
over the high wastes

On Birdhopecraig to call the wicked to repentance
In Chattlehope to call Northumberland to Scottish piety
The open air carries his words to the gathered
Preaching in clearings in the forest
That they might know the truth themselves
not needing the Latin of folios

like crab-apples scattered on a wild bank
the fine pods of heresy that fall unconsidered.

foresters setting themselves above the law
close to the Holy Ghost and far from Westminster.
Heresy steals through the high passes.
Democratic doctrines thrive in the house of rain.

In five years in a cell on the Bass Rock
he crossed the gap between the seen and the hidden
wrestled with God to end the killing in the south-west
won the gift of prophecy and the enmity of government
sent his soul out into hopes and on laws.
Salt and sweet parted to let that salmon through

3) *The Underground*
Invisible in lies where truth is criminal
Thrown into a great emptiness where sound's interminable
Making signs in darkness
Holding a white stone on our tongues, held in a chasm of spite
Scratching tablets of lead with an iron nail
the counter-signs to unmake a whole universe
in a crypt washed by a pure mineral glow
Where rival patterns of air tear leaves in mimic fight
On the margins of great empires
under hedges and in dead ground
fulfilling acoustic symmetries
cracking poisons in mended pans
Banished to a great solitude to reach perfection
Transforming what we forget
by slow breaking of fixed syllables

Altyn-Dagh

1. *The Gold Mountain at the centre of the cosmos; the beautiful child who slips from his parents' grasp*

We fly through the visible
as if on wings
hearing the arche-syllable.
As creatures of light (*roshnan*) we shun the darkness
as dwellers in air we shun what can be touched
Snared by the time caught in narratives
We watch the genres grow and decay
with the heroes caught in their scenes
Tunes for the acquisition of a body
meters moving out without words inside them

In the mountain glare
where everything is close to everything else
we apprehend colour as damage
and wonder how a bowl breaks
cracks running through its clasp
the energy taken up by the cracks.
As the sheer flux is torn into colours
we ask about
a silent erasing engulfing current
that breaks up the clear speech
lines crossing
an integral and adequate and lost extent:
as one language becomes two
hearing lost in hollows between rocks
Rules of splitting, of irreversibility. Of loss of symmetry in ingots.
Of loss of contact out of hearing.
The surface of the shear was granular,
pitted by sound

a single place splitting into four.
What fell east
became Chinese, what fell north
became Siberian, what slid south changed to
Iran, and the westward downfall
became European.

Syllables thickening the air into ridges

Spell for the decoying of a soul into a child
a single voice luring something which only wants to vanish
I don't want to
how do you like it now
Make that sound again
being drawn into the loops that always
reach their own head and return again
again sound
again sound
again sound
that persuades the child to learn words
before words can persuade it

A beautiful child is jealous of a new baby,
stops swimming towards us, thinks
I'm not going to learn this language
Slides through the warm air, eastwards

*2. He grows up in China, learns their culture, forgets their
culture, becomes alienated, and flees to another place*

After climbing down the slope to the East,
he searched for missing parts of the series
made collections of rare words
What country is this?
how many milliseconds split one sound from another?
why is the fertile land divided up as it is?
why is the West white?

He decked the trestle with crazed bowls
painting the cracks on sized bamboo strips
in series of hundreds, the inventory
of jags and forkings
where the caged heat withdrew consent

where the hollow lost its grip

Beset by false memories and sensations
he ejected what he'd learnt.
The series fell out like beads off a broken string.
He forgot who owned what
forgot who could sleep with who,
the difference between men's and women's work,
forgot the order in which sounds were joined.
Forgot why the two sides of the body don't match.
He walked out looking for silence.

*3. He is escorted by Manichaean Sogdian merchants
on one of their cyclic journeys*

Stretched thin like vapour over far ways
an open hand brings the distant into reach
of a kind of narrative walk called peddling
We know all languages and never rest
We carry tartaric cloths, the spinnings
of worms, and the sorts are
Amita Dimita Trimita
Staurax, Blattion, Katablattion
Chrysoclavus, Tyreus, Fundatum
Exarentasmata

seized by a body and losing emptiness
they seize an idea to gain emptiness

With tender hands that could wipe
the scratches from the face of coins

read in the dark
the lettering of royal luck, *khvarenah*
the cape of natal light

Taking ten per cent
on the exchange of one year for another
Nine per cent
on the exchange of summer for fruit

Delving pits for the charring of wood
to scour the grease off gold
to make the luck pristine
the meshless cape that sweeps

On the heights
you see the true emptiness,
watch from a high tower
the original pearl that fell
corroded by symbolism
to gain finitude

the pearl at the core of the brain
is the jewel we dive for
in autumns of written leaves

the uncorroded drop of white
the forms dissolving
incessant loss of memory

the act of forgetting as flying
the act of remembering
as falling
the texts on silk paper
opening the edges of the body

4.

A sound spoken in the Pamirs
is heard in the forests of Europe

Picked from the shore of a Siberian lake
the pebbles he rasps for colour to paint a bird of clay
and as he pierces it so a sound is released
that flies across the shoreless ground
deformed into a dozen shapes
by the lapping of linguistic drift
stiff wind, loose wind
that changes shape a dozen times
from *piandj* to *pyat'* to *five* to *pump*
to the final shore, the Atlantic
Oracular wind
that never stirs
the sound painted in stripes
on swept but stiff wings
of the fired bird
by the lake in Siberia

Recoil of the feather the cat swallows
bent in the gullet
and resurfacing
swallowed in two directions
— drying in a neat heap with the claws

The mountains of languages
ridges of stiffened air
with their falls that protect
fabulous and gatherable variation
relict curves of lost sounds

5. He takes refuge with the fire-worshippers of the oases; forgets
their culture, becomes alienated, and flees to another place

The Parthian provinces of the north
snows crossed by chains of buildings for travellers

closed myth cycles
drifting west
on the mouths of horsemen

going up where the birds from the Green Sea go

a soft shore where knowledge ends
and there is the vibration of water

Who built towers to catch
the light of stars falling through chill dry air
like a river poured down an infinite slope
into the world of separate forms
that look like damage

By fires they sing a lullaby
to lure the baby into its mortal body
a rigmarole of delights and savours
hanging on every bough
spinning glass to call
a rare bird onto a tree of glints
too curious to use its wings —
a visitor who asked a thousand questions
and could never leave this world again

6. He wanders to Europe, forgets their culture,
becomes alienated, and flees to another place

He forgot their language and so
walked past a culvert
with water flowing in 2 different directions

where Slavonic and Persian part,
sound cohering as its internal structure changes.
Where the marmot makes every call twice. Where the mouse
has children with two different names.
What if we carry a romance
from east to west
re-scanning the rhythmic groups
translating the form of words
twisting the asymmetries that turn
telling Parthian minstrel legends in Russian guise?

The mind that was its own environment
in the wind-still
memorized the shapes cut into the standing stone
and turned into them
settled in villages to wear the ways

At the edge of the grass
Till he came to the land covered in birch trees.
To the eaters of butter. To the women who pleased themselves.
To the mountains with the hearts of copper.
Rowed sheep out to the grass of the summer isles;
where the beaches are choked with driftwood.
Drank at the burials in boat-shaped coffins
for the pits with lynx claws, with the wings of many birds,
with the bowl of crab apples against the pull of deep winter.
Learnt the poems in alliterative metre. The braided tales
about the four red parts of the world.
He forgot their customs and their names. Forgot where to walk
as he moved in the Hercynian Forest.
Never saw the village again.

7. *He wanders north to Siberia*

On the shore of the swamp
the chest amulets clatter like brittle ice
with heroic beasts frozen in their scenes,

tarnished beasts of the lake family,
the helpful spirits.
The good-tempered cold-weather dogs keep
the mimic aggression of the guardian,
put their faith in the closeness of all to each;
wrapped with long lash-hairs
to keep ice from getting into their paw-pads,
they chase geese into the water.

The geese lashed to a sled escort the sun
under the pristine northern waters
to all the dwarf willow thickets and the fresh lakes

8. *He laments his true home on Golden Mountain where all*
forms are indeterminate

The infant tilted towards the world of sound
faces both ways, looks back from the finite
at the boundless.

And his voice said: Why should I lose
My perfect state, shattered in parts
That forget the language of all mankind
And the geometry which contains all shapes?
A message reached me from my home in the mountains
where they climb the ice with the claws of lynxes
the place equidistant from all places
where all objects have the same shape
It called me back to my family and home
where serenity is brought back by forgetting
where drops of sunlight freeze as gold
on Altyn-Dagh — the actinic mountain
where bowls of ice protect piles of fruit
without colour, glassy, shedding rays like the sun

Everyone in the high pastures was worried about me,
And they wrote me a letter.
Be mindful of the Pearl,

for whose sake you have gone down into the south.
Remember your robe of glory,
recall your splendid mantle,
Their verdant garlands never fade,
They are wreathed brightly in numberless colours.

Fingers draw cracks in the bowl of the sky
where the Serene walk, not hastening or wavering,
in white clothing, bearing tall white staves
towards the face of tangible gold

BAD
gob in a bungle. up and at'em snore
a cement-mixer being raped by a warthog.
a concrete-masher being mixed by a wart-peeler.
a book being wrapped by a Concrete Quaker.
a pigbag being snogged by a trashpile
a gadarene metaphone. a mudchute garageophone.
BOB
paper wraps coal and splits
flash exposure in bonfire ash
space folded within potato peel
textured reprowarthog print-skin
blackpowder detonation toning
steep deep scrumpled slide sides
flattened burst in high carbon relief
COB
a creeping retch. a nagging yodel.
wriggle of battered babble
a flue of flustered rubble
gerbil hacking out the burble.
splutter hoiking out the furball.
smoke throat choked with thwarts
Jackie Leroux watch your Ps and Qs
Doctor Dog, thicken your diction
BING
call the rabble to the gabble
seize the grunts from the gullets
tug the shapes from the syllables
bang your head on a tingling black bin
shove your legs down the drain
hubble rubble scrumple and cobble
Bob and Bing are two different things
gravel and Silver are two different hoarse
OB.

bad-a-bing. bob the gob.
tumble to the lurch. bang a gong.
rama lama bing cob bing
bobbledehoy. binggone.
BONG
bong. bong. bong.

Acallamh answers without the questions

Carberry Cat-head.

Pre-solar grains with exotic isotope ratios.

A language of mixed Norse and Gaelic parts.

A name for the Protestants when denied the door of human
settlements.

A size (roughly Denmark) above which nations must fall prey to
arrogance and self-deceit

By an iron-rich tissue at the base of the nose

The Caledonian for 'old-growth forest'.

From Morocco to Lisbon. Then to Galicia. Then to Brittany. Then
to Cornwall. Then to Aberystwyth. Then to Dublin.
Then to the Solway Firth.

A device in the poems of Robert Crawford.

Beech-bark prepared for writing on.

A map showing the geographical boundary where projective
identification stops, and sceptical reason starts.

Time after the arrival of class society and private ownership of land.

The migrating lakes of the Inner Asian Depression.

One of the weapons depots of the National Museum.

Artificial hills erected to strengthen the links between culture and
landscape in the works of 19th C novelists.

Lodomy, lorimer, mirligoes, gallowglass, clishmaclaver.

The Cowlairs Chord.

Sea-pedlars who translated Swedish ballads into Scots.

A set of Symboliste frescoes in a prosperous Irvingite church.

An existential decision to design the perfect steam engine although
no country was buying anything but diesel.

A name for the predominance of Orcadians in the Hudson's Bay
trading area.

The invention of solitude in Lower Egypt.

Kind of sea-fog rising when trying to match inner experience with
historical processes or family history with State narratives.

A technique of wandering Buddhist monks for repelling wild beasts
    without bloodshed.
An allegorical Highland village where post-structuralism comes true.
A three-volume collection of invective.
The walrus head conventionally supplied by prospective sons in
    law as a character reference.
A term of endearment applied to mosquitoes in the western regions.
A form of indignation expressed by walruses.
Collective noun for a gathering of communist modernist poets.
Mnemonic poem recording 30 kinds of servile status.
A form of investment in a closed period of national prosperity
    based on the destruction of neighbouring peoples.
A series of freeform doubts following from the writing of Scottish
    history by people who are not English.
The preference of cats for fishing havens.
Technique for recognising individual sheep at a distance.
Carberry Cat-head.

The twelve days of Christmas; *or,* The Return from Chaos, Bad Weather, and Marzipan

There is a legend that the universe disappears as the year ends and has to be rebuilt piece by piece during the Twelve Days of Christmas.

'Ianus habet finem: cum carmine crescit et annus.'

I
The sun has been tied to a fast sled
drawn by geese,
submerges now, northwards, in the ocean.
Far away on the damp horizon
a beautiful child is drifting away
they call the New Year
It is scared of the dark
where objects dissolve as daylight fades
into a sludge of apocalyptic collapse
where we keep light in bottles
and use alcohol to find our way around
Everything that dies some day comes back

II
This year has no name
It has no nature
It is weightless, unconscious, lifeless, and cannot feel
It knew no image
and was like that in its imagelessness
It saw no likeness
and like that it was likenessless
an eye that was unknown to flesh
and like that was flesh without light
Their bodies will look the same, front and back
neither will they be named heirs

when there is no distinction
who can inherit from another

It will measure out heaven and earth with its fingers
It will run the dust of the earth through its mouth
It will weave with lime-bast and osiers

We call on the president
to call on the Project officers
to call on Wilkinson
to get somebody told about this thing

III

Smutch by smutch moths carry darkness in their jaws
delivering it as fuel to the furnace till it blows scrolls of dark smoke
and in the wake of the ladles
tumbling flakes flare up in light.
A spigot opens in the base of the cooker:
a shining even fluid pours out in rods
to be picked up as torches
with which
thousands of silverfish
are lighting the stars one by one
they come to the sun at last
and the grey haze becomes the first day

eggs of metal spatter from the furnace brink

IV

the bronze star shoots
drawing back a curtain of light

the star
impacts in a lake of steam, a plume of sea,
hisses

the bronze egg washed up
on a coast covered with goose quills

its surface quakes and teems
black soil with a million species of bacteria waiting for the Call

the year is the circuit of a star
a very small year
is marked on the surface of an infant star
a blowing bubble-raft of eggs
where incomplete substances
are turning into honey, silver, starfish and firebrats

the egg breathes out and becomes the foreshore

At the end of a bright curve
the poet Balde digs for the shooting star
and on clearing it from Bavarian mud
finds a plane face covered with a poem
in a forgotten and rustic language.
Poesis Osca. He recognizes it as his.

V

What starts to come into view
is a crew of lubberly fiends
furry Magi bearing their gifts for the Year Child
thick-witted ravers on a royal carouse
in whom time sleeps like the weevil in the potato
Ossy, Iggy, Ranter, and Lump
grow fingers and start playing rough music
chiding and howling like a winter storm
they blow the soot back down the chimney
and shake flour all around the kitchen
they are confused and misunderstood, they are the same front
          and back
the prints in the flour have seven fingers

the trails in the soot have seven toes
a handful and a half of digits
turn out an earful of symmetry
the waits with their twelve tunes foretelling twelve months
a lumpish band blowing shinbones and cawing like rooks
fish for daylight in the swirls of darkness

You lay down your bagpipe to hear that if you answer enough
            quiz questions
you can have the gift of speech
in a café where Ida Rubinstein, Helena Rubinstein, and Jack Ruby
give you your instructions piece by piece
you memorise your lines for the role
'Lay down your weapons, rash earthling'
'But Jim, a grammar of narcissism isn't a theory"
"but Mary-Sue, circularity is not global!"
and
"I ask the masses for their permission to speak"

The child doesn't believe a word, drifts away from us

VI
The first to be unwrapped is the gift of sight
the sun drops a flock of quills stuffed with gold-dust
To slake the living eye which cannot be touched or satisfied
You invent colours for the words *cinnabar, indigo, rust,* and *snow*

You call the most squeamish of skins,
to ride on a steed the colour of air,
on a mount the colour of night, as clear as water
passing over rivers and land, valleys and hills
to satisfy itself with the extent of the visible.
The colours show the bands of the earth
painted by the geometry of two bodies,
pulsed by the slats of a lattice made of rotation.
Soaked with life by the star's gaze,
plants and animals are breeding and swelling
according to the Time for which rays are received —
green eyes of plants slaked by the non-terrestrial largesse.

VII
On the seventh day
You get to the Job Centre where John Lee Hooker, Captain Cook,
        and Bishop Spook
tell you your culture sank to the bottom of the tank
somewhere off the Carolines
in high seas in the low stretches of 49.
This taste is marzipan from Babylon
and this is the scent of an oilman.
It's all up with the way in
because you're all out and down
We're going to beat you flat till you come around.

VIII
On the eighth day we promise the gift of hearing
the first sensitive membrane of the first cell
on the ocean floor
is shaking with the vibrations which the water carries so carefully
It has to listen to all the cells
they imitate each other's states at intervals
something like a self rides the tiniest curls of the aqueous shake
and says, you can never be too pure or too connected
stretches itself out on a quivering brim
so you can listen to music scored for cicadas and mandolin

It says, if the wind blows in at your room
can you count how many leaves on the tree which rustled it

the Year Child smiles and makes the sound we make

Albanians speaking broken Somali
sell you a CD of Texan rockabilly
and tell you, It's not like it used to be

IX

You went in through the windows before finding the door-knob.
It was the first house.

Inside, everything was old although no-one had used it,
And its use had to be worked out from its wear.
A fire red in the grate needed poking.
The spaces fitted awkwardly round the small objects they mediated.
Gumboots, bags of small gravel, beer bottles,
a glazed earthenware bowl, a small book written on lead.
How was it possible to live with all these things?

With difficulty they rolled back the edges of the spaces,
Straightened the rows of bricks, made the roof slope.
Divided the year into plausible strips,
Imitated what civility they found in the mirrors.

X
        Double wings sweep the messenger in the shape of
a falcon. The sky falls out of the arrow, skimming sheets of
inanimate light. The tables of the poets who incise their poems on
plaques of meteorite: flat, shining, polished, iron, deeply bitten,
resisting blows, of extraterrestrial origin. Who mediate external
and internal in double flight. The messengers which run across
two theatres. Deflecting energy from the nearest star to burn
speech into the surface of cliffs.

Sextuple legs scurry the messenger in the shape of a silverfish.
who mediates nimble and low in rushes underneath the bath.
carrying pre-human information no-one understands any more.
deflecting energy from blotches of rotten wood to keep up old
traditions. The silverfish believe, if you blow up that patch of
halation enough you will see the face of God. And He has six legs
and a forky tail.

XI
The advice of the Lord Chancellor's Department is
that yaks should not go mousing

The advice of the Lord Chancellor's Department is
 that bats should eat winged insects.
That mice should give you the runaround.

That waves go sh shsh shshs hriffle.
that princesses should not cooperate.
That you shouldn't fuss and fight.
That you should name several minor Scandinavian peoples
and later on draft an answer to the cuckoo

The advice of the Lord Chancellor's Department is
that snakes should eat mammals, for goodness.
That snakes should detect prey by heat, in the dark.
That rivers should dig themselves beds.
That ice should act like a bridge.
To draw off the waters of Soar and let them lie flat for a while

The advice of the Lord Chancellor's Department is
that this land is your land
that this puddle is your puddle
that this clump of skeletonised teazles
is your clump of skeletonised teazles

That herons should catch eels crossways
and swallow them lengthways
To watch your footing as you open the floodgates.
That there's a little fjord we know in the Netherlands
where the cod like to gather in the Spring.
That everything is going to be all right

The advice of the Lord Chancellor's Department is
that water should reflect light
that boats should float
that dolphins should learn how to swim.
The weather does not have to rely on memory
beer should adopt the shape of the bowl
barnacles should acquire a holdfast.
That some syllables are longer than others
that there is no legislative basis for free verse
that rigmaroles should neither start nor end

XII
The small light flares up into a whole new day
Straight falls the ray, on its bands of equity
burning out the shadows and the furtive forms

Cutting along the seams and rejoining along the seams
the burst of light makes delivery of one Cosmos
shaped exactly like itself

But where light is faint,
in dapples and chequers
Chaos lingers undissolved, bronze-coloured eggs
with heaving surfaces of shapes that change
at every instant, a bell of air
very quietly teeming
with a thousand voices at once

Notes

Weapons Form With Music
There is a 13th century Chinese novel called *The Water Margin*, of which I am very fond. Mr Brian Holton translated it into Scots. This seemed like a good opportunity to write about Chinese outlaws in Scotland. Figures from Patrick Walker's *Biographia Presbyteriana* also appear. I also used some martial arts magazines.

Ghost Technology: Extreme Computing Fair
Describes an idealised research engineer, the kind of person who might have been attending the Extreme Computing Fair. Joshua Logan directed the film of *South Pacific*, with its avant-garde colour effects. The 'Orion Project' was one for nuclear-powered spacecraft, on which the physicist Freeman Dyson worked — who was at the Extreme Computing Fair.

Swimming in Spirals
The observation that frogs, carried into outer space as an experiment, swam in pure spirals, suggested that their normal courses were influenced by gravity. This inspired the notion that they could be used to detect gravity and hence the presence of nearby masses, as a navigation aid.

Blauer Reiter at Ducketts Common
There was a Turkish festival on Ducketts Common, near Turnpike Lane, with a poster which I stole by taking it off a wall. The poster shows the painted leather puppet Karagöz, who appears in the poem.

Andy-the-German
This deals with the build-up to the Oklahoma City Bombing of 1995, and with a figure known as Andy the German, who was head of security at a camp called Elohim City Compound, and is said to have been working for the German guard of the constitution, which wanted to prevent neo-Nazi propaganda from being printed in Oklahoma and distributed in Germany. The theme of

the poem is deception, and it puts forward a theory which I do not believe in.

Needwood and Charnwood
A 'national forest' is being grown, linking the two ancient forests of Needwood and Charnwood. It starts about 3 miles from the house where I grew up. Much of the area to be covered is poisoned ground, to be healed by the trees.

Mainadik Scholia
Some friends of mine had a project for filming *The Bacchae*, for which I was to provide a new translation of the Greek text. The project fell through due to an excess of ideas, but we had focussed intensely on it and I wanted to recover something from the deserted site.

Precipice of Niches
The 'x-zone' features in one theory of the origin of planets, where the 'x zone' is one where material whirling round the sun is thrown off rather than falling back in. The 'x-wind' is not made of air but of particles, thus slung into space. 'Chondrule insets' are nodules of metal in meteorites, whose make-up records the temperature of the zone where the inset was formed.

Photographing the Ideal
Describes someone attempting to take film of England in about 1942, under the aegis of Jack Beddington, who controlled all stocks of film and had specific ideas about how England was supposed to look.

Vertical Features Remake
The speaker is the pilot of a plane taking aerial photographs of a part of England.

The star temple of Sumatar Harabesi
Aby Warburg proved in 1912 that the frescoes of the Months in the Palazzo Schifanoia in Ferrara are based on the 'decans' in *Picatrix*, an astrological work written in Arabic by moon-

worshippers from Harran in Syria. In 1963 J.B. Segal visited a star-temple, with seven buildings for the seven planets, nearby — at Sumatar Harabesi. The poem is about making ideology visible. Segal has now withdrawn this identification.

Altyn-Dagh
Altyn-Dagh is a made-up name, 'gold mountain' in Turkish. In Chinese colour symbolism, gold is the colour of the centre. There are mountains called 'golden' — the Altai — in Central Asia. *Roshnan* means 'creatures of light', i.e. 'humans', in Parthian Manichaean texts. The nucleus of the poem is the idea of the undifferentiated as the precursor of all forms — the centre in the sense of being equally close to everything. I was interested in the idea of a place where Chinese, European, Iranian, and Siberian cultures touched, and of a language equally close to the languages of all those places.

Bob Cob Bing Bong
Bob Cobbing was a 'sound poet' whose sound filled me with fear and loathing. His 'photocopier art' was not half so bad.

Acallamh Answers Without the Questions
This is an old Irish genre in which one voice poses questions and another answers them. I thought to remove the questions. The reader has to decide what they were. This is a tribute to the Informationist poets. In modern Gaelic, 'acallamh' means 'interview'.

The Twelve Days
According to the argument of Dumézil's *Le mythe des Centaures*, the twelve days of Christmas were seen, by the Indo-Europeans or some descendant group, as days of chaos, a primal time, where everything reverts back to formlessness. Each day foretells the course of one month of the New Year. The universe is remade, over that time, by a group with the attributes of sovereignty, who play music; they have the forms of animals, and are associated with winter storms. Centaurs are a variety of these creatures with whom hobby-horses, tricks, and the casting of lots are associated.